Ladybird Readers

Ice Worlds

Series Editor: Sorrel Pitts
Written by Rachel Godfrey

LADYBIRD BOOKS

UK | USA | Canada | Ireland | Australia
India | New Zealand | South Africa

Ladybird Books is part of the Penguin Random House group of companies
whose addresses can be found at global.penguinrandomhouse.com.
www.penguin.co.uk   www.puffin.co.uk   www.ladybird.co.uk

Penguin
Random House
UK

First published 2018
001
Text copyright © Ladybird Books Ltd, 2018

Printed in China

A CIP catalogue record for this book is available from the British Library

ISBN: 978–0–241–31957–4

All correspondence to:
Ladybird Books
Penguin Random House Children's
80 Strand, London WC2R 0RL

MIX
Paper from
responsible sources
FSC® C018179

Ladybird Readers

BBC earth

Ice Worlds

Inspired by BBC Earth TV series and
developed with input from BBC Earth
natural history specialists

Contents

Picture words

ice

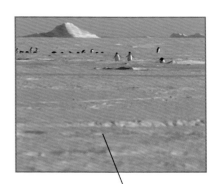

frozen ocean

land

rock

polar bear

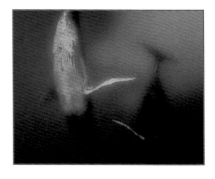

whales

stomach

Emperor penguin

seals

chick

lay (an egg)

born (verb)

7

Ice worlds

The Arctic and the Antarctic are ice worlds on Earth.

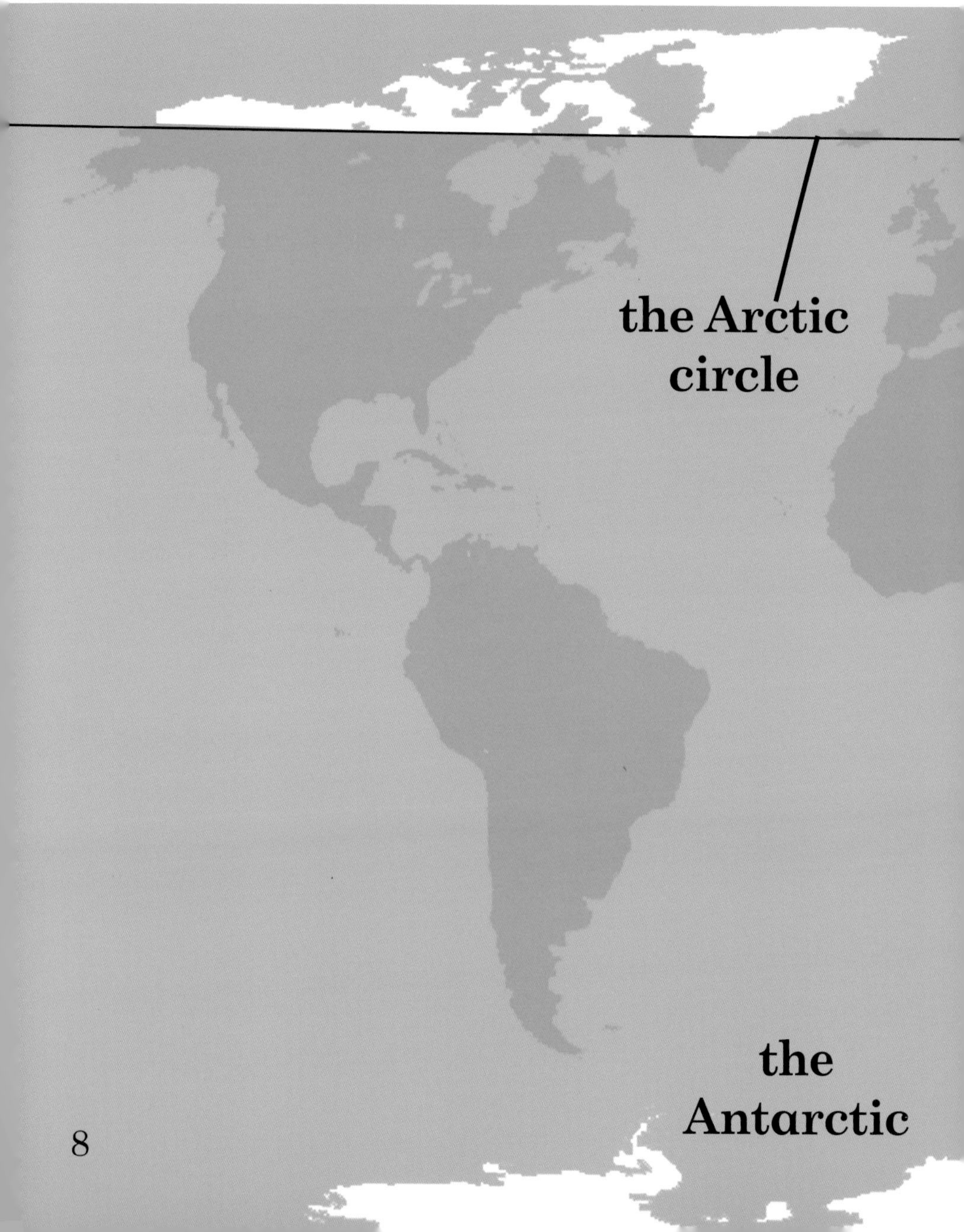

the Arctic circle

the Antarctic

The North Pole is in the Arctic, and the South Pole is in the Antarctic.

the North Pole

the South Pole

Living in the Arctic

The North Pole is in the Arctic.
It is difficult for animals
to live in the Arctic.

These animals live in the Arctic.

polar bear

Arctic wolf

Arctic hare

musk ox

walrus

Living in the Antarctic

The South Pole is in the Antarctic. It is difficult for animals to live in the Antarctic.

A lot of birds live in the Antarctic.

| snow petrel | Adelie penguin | Emperor penguin |

These animals visit the Antarctic to find food in the ocean.

whales

seals

Finding food in the Arctic

In the Arctic in winter, there's grass and other plants under the snow. Musk oxen break the hard snow with their feet to eat the grass.

Smaller birds and animals find food under the snow.

Arctic wolves eat other animals.

This wolf is watching some musk oxen.

Polar bears in spring

Mother polar bears can stay under the Arctic snow for five months in winter.

A mother polar bear comes out
from under the snow.

Her two-month-old cubs
come after her.

cubs

The mother polar bear looks after her cubs. She teaches them to walk on the snow.

It's difficult, but the cubs learn quickly.

After two weeks, the cubs can walk on the ocean ice. Now, they can look for food with their mother.

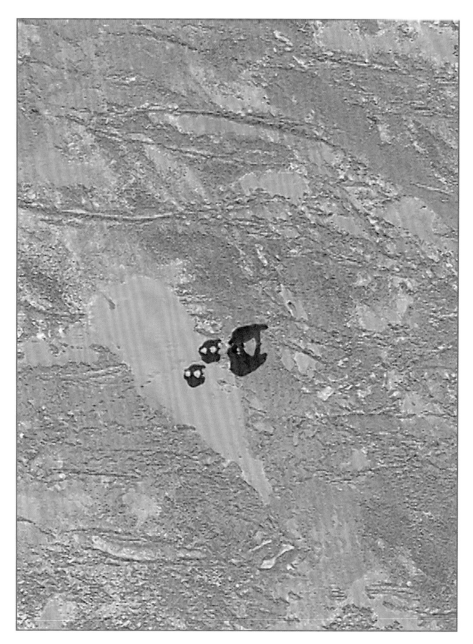

Polar bears swim alone in the cold ocean. They look for seals to eat. Seals are hard to find when the ice melts.

Their big front paws help polar bears to swim well.

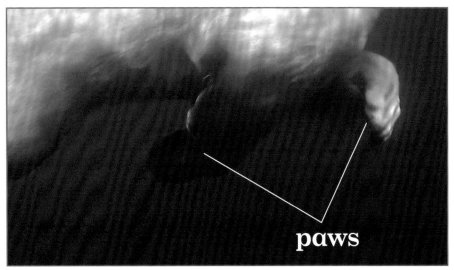

paws

After a few days in the ocean, this male polar bear sees walruses on land. He can eat a walrus.

Birds in summer

In summer, seabirds come to the Arctic to have their chicks.

chick

Little auks look like penguins, but they can fly. Little auks lay their eggs on rocks. They lay one egg each time.

little auks

The little auks must fly away from this Arctic fox, who wants to eat them.

Food in the Antarctic

In the Antarctic, the ocean is full of food. Seals and whales come here to eat.

seals

Humpback whales eat small ocean
animals called krill. They catch
the krill by making bubbles.

bubbles

The whales work together to catch the krill.

Snow petrels

Snow petrels lay their eggs on rocks in the Antarctic.

They eat fish and krill from the ocean.

Snow petrels are white with black beaks and black eyes. They clean their feathers in the snow.

feather

Emperor penguins

In winter, Emperor penguins come up on to the ice in the Antarctic.

Sometimes, the Emperor penguins walk.
Sometimes, they travel on their stomachs.

The Emperor penguins
meet here. It is where
they all have their chicks.

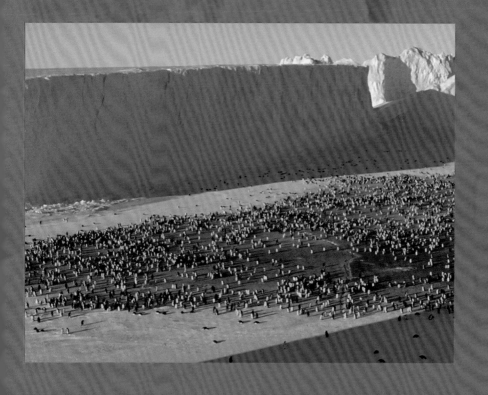

Starting a family

Female and male penguins make pairs.

The mother penguin lays an egg.

After this, she's very tired. She gives the egg to the father penguin.

Moving the egg

1. It's very cold. The father must quickly take the egg from the mother.

2. The father uses his beak to move the egg towards him.

egg

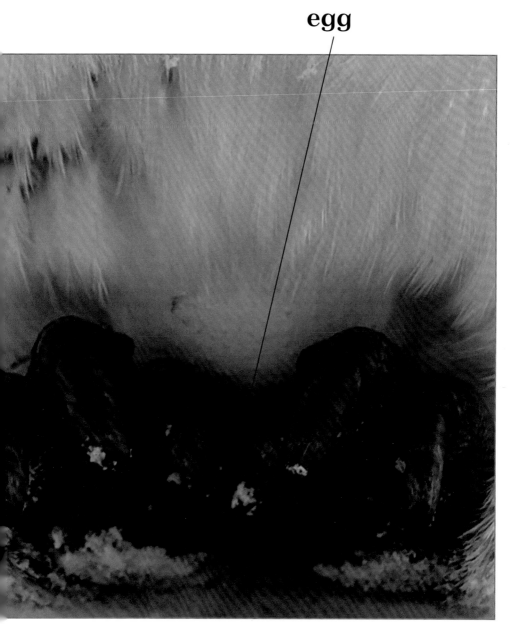

3. Now, the egg is safe and warm
with the father.

A long, cold winter

The mother penguins travel to the ocean again to look for food. A long, cold winter is coming. The sun stays down.

The father penguins stay together on the ice with their eggs. They don't eat for almost four months.

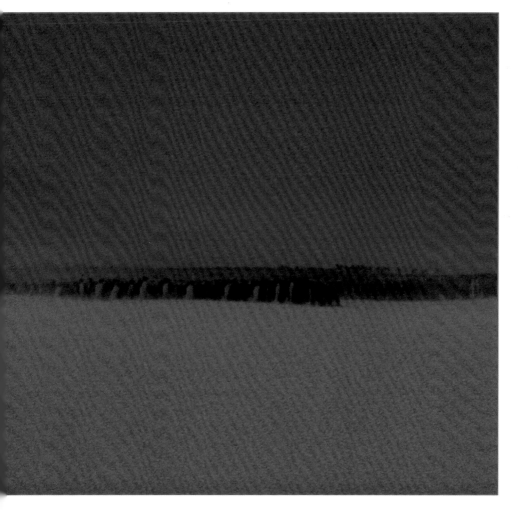

It is very dark in the Antarctic in winter.

The chicks come out

After many dark days, the sun comes up again.

The chicks are born. The fathers and chicks need to eat.

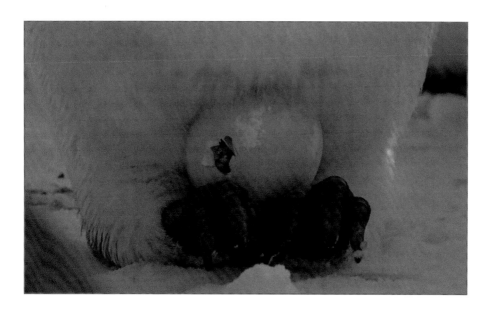

The mothers come back

The mother penguins come back from the ocean with their stomachs full of fish.

The mother penguins see their chicks for the first time.

In early summer, the chicks are ready to go into the world.

Problems for our ice worlds

The ocean ice in the Arctic is getting smaller, because our planet is getting warmer. We are losing the ice that animals need to live.

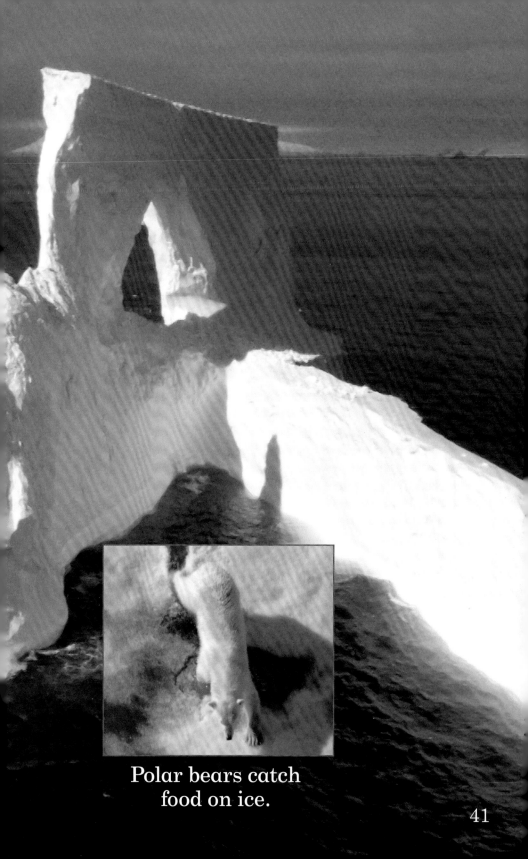

Polar bears catch
food on ice.

Our ice worlds are important

We must stop our ice worlds from getting warmer, to help the animals that live there. People need the ice worlds, too.

We can help. We can try not to use our cars. We can recycle more.

Activities

The key below describes the skills practiced in each activity.

Spelling and writing

Reading

Speaking

Critical thinking

Preparation for the Cambridge Young Learners exams

1 Look and read. Put a ☑ or a ☒ in the boxes.

1  This is rock. ☒

2 This is a polar bear.

3  This is a chick.

4  This is ice.

5  These are whales.

2 Circle the correct words.

1 The **North Pole** / **South Pole** is in the Arctic.

2 It is **difficult** / **easy** for animals to live in the Arctic.

3 Arctic wolves and **penguins** / **hares** live in the Arctic.

4 The **North Pole** / **South Pole** is in the Antarctic.

5 Animals visit the Antarctic to find **water.** / **food.**

3 Look, match, and write the words.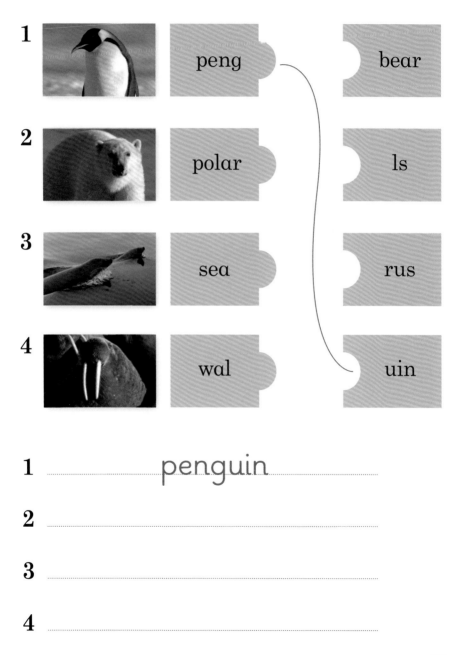

1 peng — uin — bear

2 polar — ls

3 sea — rus

4 wal — uin

1   penguin

2

3

4

4 **Read the sentences. Write the correct words.** 📖 ✏️ ✻

grass	food	animals	feet

1 There is ⎯⎯⎯ grass ⎯⎯⎯ under the snow in the Arctic.

2 Musk oxen break the hard snow with their ⎯⎯⎯⎯⎯⎯⎯⎯. Then, they eat the grass.

3 Smaller animals find ⎯⎯⎯⎯⎯⎯⎯⎯ under the snow.

4 Arctic wolves eat other ⎯⎯⎯⎯⎯⎯⎯⎯.

5 Order the story. Write 1—5.

.... Her cubs come out after her.

...1... A mother polar bear comes out from under the Arctic snow.

.... Now, the cubs can look for food.

.... It's difficult, but the cubs learn quickly.

.... The mother bear teaches the cubs to walk on the snow.

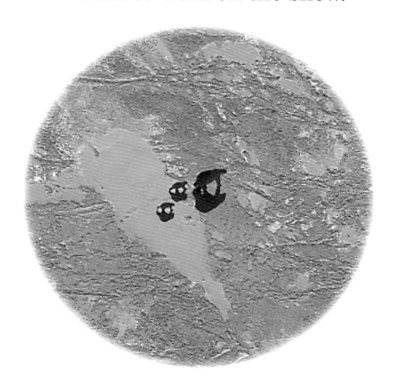

6 Circle the correct sentences.

1
a This is a mother polar bear.
b This is a cub.

2
a It's easy for the cubs to walk on the snow.
b It's difficult for the cubs to walk on the snow.

3
a The mother bear helps the cubs to walk on the snow.
b The mother bear can't help the cubs to walk on the snow.

4
a It's difficult, but the cubs learn quickly.
b It's difficult, and the cubs learn slowly.

7 Look and read. Write *yes* or *no*.

Polar bears swim alone in the cold ocean. They look for seals to eat. Seals are hard to find when the ice melts.

After a few days in the ocean, this male polar bear sees walruses on land. He can eat a walrus.

Their big front paws help polar bears to swim well.

paws

20

21

1 Polar bears swim together. ....no............

2 Polar bears eat walruses. ....

3 It is easy to find seals
when the ice melts. ....

4 Polar bears use their big
front paws to swim. ....

5 Polar bears find walruses
in the sea. ....

8 **Write the past tense of the verbs.**

1 These birds are little auks. They **(fly)**
    flew to the Arctic last summer.

2 They **(lay)** _____ their eggs
  on rocks.

3 An Arctic fox **(want)** _____
  to eat these little auks.

4 The little auks **(have)** _____
  to fly away.

9 Find the words.

```
t  s  e  w  h  a  l  e  i  l
o  e  s  h  u  b  j  l  k  k
g  d  e  i  m  n  w  i  r  u
e  f  a  f  p  m  a  k  i  h
t  o  l  g  b  u  b  b  l  e
h  o  g  c  a  t  c  h  l  t
e  d  k  s  c  b  d  r  w  l
r  b  c  e  k  u  s  i  s  l
```

seal   whale   krill   humpback

bubble   food   catch   together

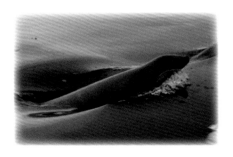

10 Ask and answer the questions with a friend.

Snow petrels

Snow petrels lay their eggs on rocks in the Antarctic.

They eat fish and krill from the ocean.

Snow petrels are white with black beaks and black eyes. They clean their feathers in the snow.

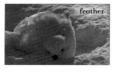

feather

27

1

> *What are these birds?*

> *They are snow petrels.*

2 Where do they lay their eggs?

3 What do they eat?

4 How do they clean their feathers?

11 Choose the correct answers.

1 Emperor penguins come up on to the ice in . . .

a the Arctic. **b** the Antarctic.

2 The Emperor penguins come up on to the ice in . . .

a summer. **b** winter.

3 Sometimes, they travel on their . . .

a heads. **b** stomachs.

4 All the Emperor penguins have their chicks in . . .

a different places.

b the same place.

12 **Complete the sentences.
Write a—d.**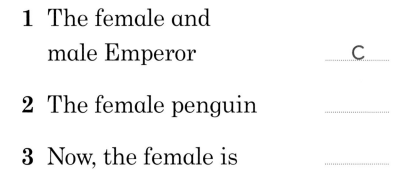

1 The female and
male Emperor .... c ....

2 The female penguin ....

3 Now, the female is ....

4 The female gives the ....

a lays an egg.

b egg to the father.

c penguins make pairs.

d very tired.

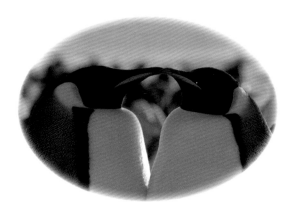

13 **Read the sentences. Choose the correct words, and write them on the lines.** 📖 ✏️ ✿

> **1** cold   colder   a cold
>
> **2** quick   quicker   quickly
>
> **3** body   beak   feet
>
> **4** safely   safe   safest

1 It is very _____cold_____ in

the Antarctic.

2 The father must _____

take the egg.

3 The father uses his

_____ to move the egg.

4 Now, the egg is _____

and warm.

57

14 **Read the answers.**
Write the questions.

1 Where does the mother

penguin travel to?

She travels to the ocean again.

2 ....

....

She travels to the ocean to look for food.

3 ....

....

He stays on the ice with the egg.

15 Choose the correct words and write them on the lines. 📖 ✏️ ⭐

| be born | lay (an egg) | chick | Emperor penguin |

1 This bird has its babies in the Antarctic.

Emperor penguin

2 When an egg comes out of a mother penguin.

3 When a baby penguin comes out of an egg.

4 This is a baby penguin.

16 Match the two parts of the sentences. Then, write them on the lines. 📖 ✏️

1 The mothers come back

2 They see their chicks

3 The chicks go into the world

a for the first time.

b in early summer.

c with their stomachs full of fish.

1 The mothers come back with their stomachs full of fish.

2

3

17 Talk to a friend about the problems in the ice worlds. 💬 ❓

1 *Why is the ocean ice in the Arctic getting smaller?*

Because our planet is getting warmer.

2 Why is this a problem for polar bears, do you think?

3 What can we do to help?

18 **Write the sentences.** 📖 ✏️

1 is · smaller · The · ocean · ice · getting · . · Arctic · the · in

The ocean ice in the Arctic is getting smaller.

2 catch · on · Polar bears · seals · ice · .

3 must · planet · our · stop · We · warmer · getting · .

19 **Write about your favorite animal from the Arctic or the Antarctic. Why is it your favorite?** ✏ ❓

My favorite animal from

Level 3

Sharks

978–0–241–25382–3 ☐

The Jungle Book

978–0–241–25383–0 ☐

The Red Knight

978–0–241–25384–7 ☐

The Elves and the Shoemaker

978–0–241–25385–4 ☐

Rapunzel

978–0–241–28394–3 ☐

Great Buildings

978–0–241–28400–1 ☐

Minibeasts

978–0–241–28404–9 ☐

Puss in Boots

978–0–241–28407–0 ☐

Jack and the Beanstalk

978–0–241–28397–4 ☐

Hansel and Gretel

978–0–241–29861–9 ☐

The Talent Show

978–0–241–29859–6 ☐

A Great Night!

978–0–241–29863–3 ☐

Bumblebee and the Rock Concert

978-0-241-29867-1 ☐

Where Animals Live

978-0-241-29868-8 ☐

Snow White and the Seven Dwarfs

978-0-241-31955-0 ☐

Ice Worlds

978-0-241-31957-4 ☐

The Pony School News

978-0-241-31956-7 ☐

Now you're ready for Level 4!